ANALYZE PEOPLE

By Harvey Stuarts

Copyright © 2017 by Harvey Stuarts

The trademarks that are used are without any consent, and the publication of the trademark is without permission or backing by the trademark owner. All trademarks and brands within this book are for clarifying purposes only and are the owned by the owners themselves, not affiliated with this document.

Disclaimer and Terms of Use: The Author and Publisher has strived to be as accurate and complete as possible in the creation of this book, notwithstanding the fact that he does not warrant or represent at any time that the contents within are accurate due to the rapidly changing nature of the Internet. While all attempts have been made to verify information provided in this publication, the Author and Publisher assumes no responsibility for errors, omissions, or contrary interpretation of the subject matter herein.

Any perceived slights of specific persons, peoples, or organizations are unintentional. In practical advice books, like anything else in life, there are no guarantees of results. Readers are cautioned to rely on their own judgment about their individual circumstances and act accordingly.

This book is not intended for use as a source of legal, medical, business, accounting or financial advice. All readers are advised to seek services of competent professionals in the legal, medical, business, accounting, and finance fields.

TABLE OF CONTENTS

INTRODUCTION

The first time I saw Sarah, not a real name, I noticed that she was only accompanying guys. I also noticed that she was talking about guy related topics and enjoying the talk so much.

For a normal girl such a conversation would have been so boring but for Sarah things were different. The first thing I concluded about her when I analyzed her behavior is that she doesn't like her feminine role and that's why she is trying to assume another role for herself.

When I collected further information I discovered that she was raised in a house that elevated the value of a man so much and degraded the value of women and that's why she started protesting against her gender. One extremely important factor you must notice when analyzing people's behavior is to understand how they were brought up at home since childhood experiences can permanently affect someone's future behavior.

One day I heard her saying that she is extremely interested in zodiac signs. As i said once that our interest in a subject is determined by our desire to compensate for the things we lack. Because Sarah lacked selfunderstanding she developed a strong interest in zodiac signs so that she can compensate for her lack of knowledge about herself.

One important thing to note when analyzing someone's behavior is that people move in the direction that allows them to compensate for their perceived weaknesses.

Sarah Was extremely competitive and always used to challenge people whenever possible. I concluded that she was the youngest kid in the family and I was right. The youngest kid always finds himself surrounded by more capable grown ups and siblings and thus becomes extremely competitive to compensate for his weakness.

When you analyze someone's behavior you should also relate it to his birth order.

One weird thing I noticed about Sarah is that even though she was competitive, extroverted and strong willed she got married to a guy who was shy, reserved and not that confident.

That further proves our analysis true. Sarah hated being a woman because she was taught that all women are weak and less important than men. Later on she only got attracted to weak men because that would give her the chance to become the dominant member in the family.

The final important note about analyzing people's behavior is that most people are never aware of the dynamics of their personality. Sarah was never aware of the reason that got her attracted to weak men because all of that happens on the unconscious level.

This book will help you to be a master in understanding and analyzing people's behaviour.

DIFFERENT PERSONALITY TYPES

Your dreams talk about psychological problems that you can notice in your mind and behavior. They also talk about life situations that are worrying you all the time. There is a strong connection between your dreams and your life.

Your dreams give you information about everything that is important for you. You learn how to successfully solve your problems and find sound mental health.

You need psychotherapy even if you believe that you are a sensible person. You have inherited absurdity into your anti- conscience, which is your wild conscience. You cannot see or control this primitive content, but it is active inside you. You dream exactly because you need the unconscious guidance in order to eliminate your anti-conscience. You have to tame your wild nature and transform it into human nature.

The unconscious mind analyzes your psychological system, your daily life, your past, your behavior, your reality, and many other details. You understand who you really are, and you verify that there is a previously traced destiny for you. Your destiny is based on your psychological type because it defines your behavior.

If you'll logically think about this matter you will understand that it makes sense, since you have inherited absurdity in your brain and psyche, and since you must develop your intelligence. Your life must be organized in a way that will help you positively transform your personality, and avoid making the mistakes of your psychological type. This is how you'll have the chance to evolve.

Each of us are different in many ways and that fact cannot possible be disputed by anyone who has any back ground in the human sciences, as it has been scientifically proven that we all have unique finger prints, DNA, hair, looks, behavior and facial expressions and the combination of these things make us unique "personality types" so to speak. We also function from two different perspectives and we need to understand how each one of us functions. We each like to think that we are special (which we are) and in that portrayal system, we mostly portray what we perceive we want people to think about us. On the other side of the coin we have a reality in what we truly believe about ourselves and the way we feel inwardly. Many of us become disillusioned with our true inner picture, simple because of a misunderstanding of our personal purpose in life.

The fact that we allow this dissatisfaction to creep into our lives, we create an inner insecurity within ourselves and we then start looking at others or alternatively we start behaving like others, which is completely outside our true personality, thereby attempting to look different, behave different, think different, dress different and when looking at our big picture, become dissatisfied with our true personality, allowing society to name us as a "personality type" which is definitely going to influence our level to be successful in life. Society has made us believe that we need to conform to a standard of behavior, which then classifies us into various but different personality types, which seems impossible to escape from, due to the social pressures placed on society by those who wish to control our lives.

This type of personality manipulation is starting at a very young age in this modern time, where young boys or girls are given labels, commonly known as Attention Deficit Disorder (ADD) or alternatively, Attention Deficit Hyperactive Disorder (ADHD). This immediately creates a personality label which has been proven through research conducted by the author and many other scholars, to be false and completely far from the true reality. The fact that each one of us are uniquely different and those different likes or dislikes and different beliefs between good and bad or alternatively right or wrong, and at the same time have many different talents in different areas. Should we be in school and have little interest in the subjects being taught, our attention span in the subject would be very short, making the ability to concentrate on the subject virtually impossible. This does not mean that there is something wrong with us as unique individuals, it only means that we have no interest in the subject and therefore have nothing to motivate us in order to pay attention.

We then start filling that time with some other activity to keep ourselves amused or occupied and more often than not disrupt the attention of others who have an interest in the subject. This behavior is then interpreted as a mental disorder of sorts namely ADHD, which in reality is totally a false perception. We have to consider such behavior as being disruptive and it would make a teachers life difficult, however, that does not mean that our personality type is wrong and therefore by creating such labels as being stupid, disobedient, impossible, lazy, et cetera, does not make our personality type, a mental disorder of any kind which was handed out by a third parties perception, who really does not have a clue what our real motivating fields of interest are at the outset.

These labels create a lot of inner insecurity as we are led to believe from the supposedly experts that there is something radically wrong with us, creating a sense of feelings that are different to others making our behavior unacceptable and improper. Our self-perceptions are moved in such a way that we desire recognition for who we really are and we then start looking at others, who may have different areas of talents, creating a desire to be just like them. These individuals are looked upon as "Stars" and hero's with envy. This leads us into attempting to look like them, and act like them which is completely contradictory to our own personality. By trying to change those inner characteristics, which results in us becoming or entering into a state of dysfunctionality, whereby our self-esteem degenerates while attempting to take on the personality of those perceived stars or personality types. We will never be able to do that successfully unless we have the right personality values or talents that are similar to those stars, leading us into creating escape mechanism such as smoking, drinking and or drugging, which seems to help us escape from the reality for a very short time, resulting with us having to deal with the reality after a brief few hours once again, resulting in a spiral decline in our ability to cope with acting out in a behavior or a personality which really is not who we are and thereby inhibiting our true personality to manifest itself, in order to live a truly satisfied and fulfilled life-style.

It is critical for each of us to understand our true unique inner talents and concentrate on those strengths and talents rather than being led into a trap, of being labelled as a personality type. Many millions of different individuals are struggling with their self-image and esteem all due to the social pressures through advertising, movies and various other social media, where they have created ideals of who we should be, and what we should dress like and look like to be socially acceptable. The biggest question that has remained unanswered for decades now is: Who set the standards for a personality type and who judges that personality type, against what criteria?

Should one have been labelled as a Personality type and one does not meet that criteria, whatever that criteria may be, it will definitely have a negative influence on your level of success in your life. In order to live a fulfilled life-style follow your passions and dreams and do not let anyone persuade you into believing that you have to comply with others opinions and beliefs in order to fulfill the role as a personality type.

THE DIFFERENT PERSONALITY TYPES

ISTJ - THE DUTY FULFILLER

Serious and quiet, interested in security and peaceful living. Extremely thorough, responsible, and dependable. Well- developed powers of concentration. Usually interested in supporting and promoting traditions and establishments. Well-organized and hard working, they work steadily towards identified goals. They can usually accomplish any task once they have set their mind to it.

ISTP - THE MECHANIC

Quiet and reserved, interested in how and why things work. Excellent skills with mechanical things. Risk-takers who they live for the moment. Usually interested in and talented at extreme sports. Uncomplicated in their desires. Loyal to their peers and to their internal value systems, but not overly concerned with respecting laws and rules if they get in the way of getting something done. Detached and analytical, they excel at finding solutions to practical problems.

ISFJ - THE NURTURER

Quiet, kind, and conscientious. Can be depended on to follow through. Usually puts the needs of others above their own needs. Stable and practical, they value security and traditions. Well-developed sense of space and function. Rich inner world of observations about people. Extremely perceptive of other's feelings. Interested in serving others.

ISFP - THE ARTIST

Quiet, serious, sensitive and kind. Do not like conflict, and not likely to do things which may generate conflict. Loyal and faithful. Extremely well-developed senses, and aesthetic appreciation for beauty. Not interested in leading or controlling others. Flexible and open-minded. Likely to be original and creative. Enjoy the present moment.

INFJ - THE PROTECTOR

Quietly forceful, original, and sensitive. Tend to stick to things until they are done. Extremely intuitive about people, and concerned for their feelings. Well-developed value systems which they strictly adhere to. Well-respected for their perserverence in doing the right thing. Likely to be individualistic, rather than leading or following.

INFP - THE IDEALIST

Quiet, reflective, and idealistic. Interested in serving humanity. Well-developed value system, which they strive to live in accordance with. Extremely loyal. Adaptable and laid-back unless a strongly-held value is threatened. Usually talented writers. Mentally quick, and able to see possibilities. Interested in understanding and helping people.

INTJ - THE SCIENTIST

Independent, original, analytical, and determined. Have an exceptional ability to turn theories into solid plans of action. Highly value knowledge, competence, and structure. Driven to derive meaning from their visions. Long-range thinkers. Have very high standards for their performance, and the performance of others. Natural leaders, but will follow if they trust existing leaders.

INTP - THE THINKER

Logical, original, creative thinkers. Can become very excited about theories and ideas. Exceptionally capable and driven to turn theories into clear understandings. Highly value knowledge, competence and logic. Quiet and reserved, hard to get to know well. Individualistic, having no interest in leading or following others.

ESTP - THE DOER

Friendly, adaptable, action-oriented. "Doers" who are focused on immediate results. Living in the here-and-now, they're risk- takers who live fast-paced lifestyles. Impatient with long explanations. Extremely loyal to their peers, but not usually respectful of laws and rules if they get in the way of getting things done. Great people skills.

ESTJ - THE GUARDIAN

Practical, traditional, and organized. Likely to be athletic. Not interested in theory or abstraction unless they see the practical application. Have clear visions of the way things should be. Loyal and hard-working. Like to be in charge. Exceptionally capable in organizing and running activities. "Good citizens" who value security and peaceful living.

ESFP - THE PERFORMER

People-oriented and fun-loving, they make things more fun for others by their enjoyment. Living for the moment, they love new experiences. They dislike theory and impersonal analysis. Interested in serving others. Likely to be the center of attention in social situations. Well-developed common sense and practical ability.

ESFJ - THE CAREGIVER

Warm-hearted, popular, and conscientious. Tend to put the needs of others over their own needs. Feel strong sense of responsibility and duty. Value traditions and security. Interested in serving others. Need positive reinforcement to feel good about themselves. Well-developed sense of space and function.

ENFP - THE INSPIRER

Enthusiastic, idealistic, and creative. Able to do almost anything that interests them. Great people skills. Need to live life in accordance with their inner values. Excited by new ideas, but bored with details. Open-minded and flexible, with a broad range of interests and abilities.

ENFJ - THE GIVER

Popular and sensitive, with outstanding people skills. Externally focused, with real concern for how others think and feel. Usually dislike being alone. They see everything from the human angle, and dislike impersonal analysis. Very effective at managing people issues, and leading group discussions. Interested in serving others, and probably place the needs of others over their own needs.

ENTP - THE VISIONARY

Creative, resourceful, and intellectually quick. Good at a broad range of things. Enjoy debating issues, and may be into "one-up-manship". They get very excited about new ideas and projects, but may neglect the more routine aspects of life.

Generally outspoken and assertive. They enjoy people and are stimulating company. Excellent ability to understand concepts and apply logic to find solutions.

ENTJ - THE EXECUTIVE

Assertive and outspoken - they are driven to lead. Excellent ability to understand difficult organizational problems and create solid solutions. Intelligent and well-informed, they usually excel at public speaking. They value knowledge and competence, and usually have little patience with inefficiency or disorganization.

BEHAVIOR PATTERNS - REAL CHANGE THAT LASTS

It is essential to release our limiting beliefs. We must clear these thoughts away before we can experience and know our True Identity. However, we must also consciously integrate our healing and transformation into our behavior and become conscious when old patterns start to re-emerge as the result of the triggering of new egoic pockets. In this section one idea will be presented at a time. It is suggested that you consciously work with this insight for a week or two before moving on to a new idea.

JUDGMENT VS DISCERNMENT

Judgment is a function performed by the ego-mind. The Whole-mind is incapable of judgment. So, when we judge we lose our Whole-minded, God connection. We trade this for whatever ego benefits we might get like: feeling superior, being angry, hating and its accompanying excitement, getting to feel separate and therefore seemingly safe, etc.. Judgment occurs when we confuse a person or ourselves with an action that the ego is engaged in. For example: we might have been told or have said, "You're a bad boy or girl for doing that." Or, we might think he or she is a terrible person because they are a cheat, a thief, or a drug addict.

Judgment occurs when we look at something or ourselves and react against it based on our past. This might include: excess weight, skin color, dress, riches or poverty, personal beliefs, etc.. In these cases we are projecting our egoic prejudices and reacting to our own limiting beliefs. We have gotten lost in the form and failed to see the real person who stands behind the form like a light bulb stands behind a lampshade. We have looked with our mind rather than our heart and as a result we have lost our connection to Source, and therefore what is really valuable.

Discernment, however, is not of the ego. It says, "This person (or myself) is engaged in a behavior in which I don't wish to participate. I can still love you or myself and not participate in the behavior. I separate you from the behavior. I see not a bad person but a person engaged in something I don't wish to be part of. I don't even have to conclude that you shouldn't be part of it. I could hold the thought that I am not able to tell if this action will, in the long run, aid or harm your growth. But, I know that for myself it is not what I want.

Discernment says, "I don't choose this, but I love you." Spiritually, we are not required to like or change anyone, just Love everyone. As we grow and transform we must discern. We must let our inner guidance tell us what to do and what to avoid. This is not judgment. This is discernment and it must occur. Do not back away from this out of fear that you are becoming judgmental.

BEHAVIORAL PATTERNS IN YOUR LEARNING MECHANISM

The famed biologist and behaviorist Konrand Lorenz (Nobel Prize laureate) and several other biologists studied human and animal behavior and concluded that the human being is pre-conditioned to behave in a certain fashion according to environmental stimuli, like all the wild animals.

There are pre-programmed behavioral patterns that start functioning when the right stimuli appear in the environment of the organism. These behavioral patterns are designed to provide the indispensable automatic reactions for survival; otherwise, the organism would die at its first attempt to abandon the nest. The behavioral patterns have several functions depending upon the animal's species and its necessities.

Many researches made by a group of biologists with several wild animals clearly revealed that the animals already know what they must do even before they are born, even without observing any other animal of the same species doing the same movements. Their movements are precise from the very first moment. A young wild animal is able to successfully kill its prey at its first attempt, by following the exact same sequence of precise movements as if it were experienced, even if it grows up isolated from other animals of its species.

When Konrand Lorenz wrote the last chapter of his book: "Behind the Mirror," where he clearly showed the existence of many behavioral patterns in the learning mechanism of the human being, he promised to write some day another book where he would show us where we can find a characteristic in the human being that is completely independent of any pattern and is responsible for the human personality.

The conclusions of his long research were quite disappointing regarding the creativity and the capacity to learn in the human being.

He really wanted to discover freedom in our cognitive mechanism, but it was very difficult to find it with the existence of so many behavioral patterns.

TO ERR IS HUMAN (AND YOU'RE HUMAN TOO!)

To err is human, to forgive divine." (Alexander Pope)

We've all heard this before...and it seems pretty straightforward. When someone makes a mistake (as we all do from time to time), we understand that it's natural to do so. And we forgive them.

Ahhh, but what about when YOU make the mistake? Do you give yourself the same latitude and leeway that you give another, or are you harder on yourself? Do you forgive yourself as quickly as you forgive another, or do you hold onto it longer?

Most of us are tougher on ourselves when we err, than we are on others. We tend to hold ourselves to a higher standard, and tend to not give ourselves the same slack we allot to others. But why should this be?

Honestly, if you love yourself, you would be just as kind, just as gentle, just as understanding with yourself as you are with others. So why aren't you?

What if, starting today, you give yourself the same compassion, the same empathy, the same acceptance that you normally offer to others? What would that look like?

Well, it might look like this: I made a mistake. I am aware of my mistake. I feel regretful that it happened, and yet I realize that my intentions were good, and it was an honest mistake. I apologize to anyone involved, and look for a solution, if warranted.

I feel any emotions that come up (embarrassment, sadness, remorse, etc.) I make a mental note to learn from this experience. And then, I let it go. I move on. (In other words, I don't dwell on it, I don't beat myself up over it, I don't stay in a place of sadness or regret.)

Imagine what it would feel like to learn from your mistake and just move on with your day? It would be amazing....a totally different experience than we're accustomed to. And suddenly, mistakes wouldn't be so traumatic, so burdensome or so heavy.

I encourage you to try this the next time you stumble or trip up. And notice how differently you feel afterwards. Notice how quickly you're able to return to an emotionally calm place - how easily you are able to restore your inner peace.

And yet, you STILL got the lesson from the experience - -that's the beauty of it!

The itch to let him know as to what went into others' pockets drove the two-legged thing crazy. Amongst tens of thousands of the beasts-of-the field, the fowl-of-the-air and the fish-of-the-sea, the homosapiens stood tense, fidgeting and biting nails. It was his turn to receive his share and therefore he was on tenterhooks.

'My! What if it is less than what the wretched canine got'?

As the thinking-reed inched his way to get his share, the stentorian voice thundered.

'Thou shalt live to see three hundred full moons.'

'Only three hundred full moons, My lord!'

'Ain't they sufficient; O'quintessence of dust?'

'May I beg my Lord, Most Gracious, to bless Thy servant with a couple more hundred of full moons!'

'In that case thou shalt go to fellow beasts and fowls.'

The idiosyncrasy (to live longer) brought the Nature's sole mistake to pachyderms, carnivores and feathered friends, denizens of the deep, arthropods and so many others. He was on the lookout for some one willing to dole out some of its lifetime in his favour. Its long antennae shot up as the short-legged creature lent an ear to the gripes of the naked-ape. Without hesitation the former parted with a fair chunk of his quota of life. The unfeathered two-legged thing was excited. He could now live to see a couple more hundreds of full moons.

But then it hardly satisfied his greed. In the frenzy of his desire to cheat death, the biped made obligatory rounds (with his begging bowl) of yet other potential donors. The otherwise greedy dog licked its master's feet and heard him patiently and sympathetically. It gifted away some period of its existence ditto-fellow beast, the 'silly donkey'. Nocturnal, wise but shy owl looked kindly upon the request of the plume-less-genus-of- bipeds and was last to dole out a hundred and odd full moons of its life.

Out of the stockpile of the life years bestowed on the humans originally by the 'Creator', it is during the first 25-30 years (he lives to see about 300 full moons) he works solely for himself. For the next 25-30 years (he lives to see about 300 full moons), gifted away by the 'silly donkey', he sweats and slaves and works his head off for others (viz, wife, children and so on).

During the life years bestowed on by the greedy dog (he lives to see about 300 full moons) he barks.

He keeps a dog watch and baby sits his grand children while his son and the daughter-in-law are away on work. And finally when he is at the death's door (the life years donated by the wise owl) he is blinded. His glassy eyes can't see therefore (he) remains unattended in the narrow dark crevices. In this part of world and the social set up the life goes like that till he dies his death.

SPEAKING AND LISTENING SKILLS

A process improvement team is from the beginning a team of investigators. They investigate process performance by looking for improvement opportunities and the root causes of problems. All of us have seen detective programs on TV where a sleuth investigates a crime. They ask questions, listen, set up stakeouts, and eventually discover what really happened. Process improvement teams follow the same strategy. They ask questions, listen, and monitor processes. All of this to discover the root causes of process problems.

An improvement team will use all four basic communication skills: reading, writing, listening, and speaking. These skills become the lubrication that allows a diverse group of team members to work through an improvement project successfully.

We are taught early and often in school to read and write while constantly being told, not taught, to listen. The result is that we are generally poor listeners. If you are not a good listener, you will miss much in life.

In the case of a process improvement project, asking questions and listening will take up the bulk of your time. In fact, listening skills may be more important than your statistical prowess. Much of the contextual information surrounding a process will be obtained through interviews and simply listening to the "shoptalk" of process owners.

Here is an exercise to help develop listening skills. The next time you are at a group function like a party or meeting, try not talking about yourself. Instead, try to learn specific and detailed information about as many people as possible. This will require you to listen carefully and ask many questions. It will not be hard, because people like to talk about themselves. All you have to do is be quiet and listen. The next time you interact with these people, you will be in a superior knowledge position because you will know a great deal about them, but they will not know much about you.

Getting the support and resources necessary to move forward in an improvement project also requires well-developed speaking skills. This is because of the need to ask questions and to tell the process' story. The best discoveries and ideas in the world are worthless if they cannot be expressed to others.

Here is an exercise that will help improve speaking skills. The next time you have a presentation to make, videotape yourself giving the presentation beforehand. When you view and listen to it, you will see and hear what others see and hear when you are speaking. You will find that you neither look nor sound like you might have thought. With this visual and audio information, you can make adjustments and increase your chances of a successful outcome.

Additionally, successful public speaking involves subject matter knowledge, good diction, projection, and some knowledge of the target audience. All of these boil down to being prepared. You must know what message you want to deliver and what terminology your audience is used to hearing. You must also anticipate the questions that will be asked and what personal motivations will be in play. A prepared speaker will know how to answer these questions and what threshold of value will be needed to sell the audience members. This way, the presentation will speak with its own merits and not be held up by the skill of the presenter.

Good diction and pronunciation are a matter of practice and feedback. Listening to yourself and getting the feedback of a test audience will be of great value. As far as pronunciation goes, make good use of a dictionary. Don't make the mistake of having your audience thinking about how you mispronounced a word rather than the merits of your business case. It is also a good idea to use words that you are comfortable using everyday. Trying to impress by using big words that are not generally part of your vocabulary will trip you up.

Projection involves two things: speaking loud enough to be heard without being too loud and speaking with conviction. You should know the layout of the room where the presentation is to take place and what audio or visual aids will be available. A strong confident voice will go long way to building and conveying conviction. Not sounding confident or being difficult to hear will be like blood in the water to the sharks that are looking for a reason to not provide the resources you need in order to be successful with your project.

Lastly, the knowledge of who your audience is and what their value prepositions are is critical. Do not forget that you are trying to motivate them to action on behalf of your project. This means that you will need to frame your presentation around their interests. A little research ahead of time before you build the presentation can give you this information.

All of the above is meaningless if you do not believe in what you are doing. Participating on an improvement team for political reasons is unproductive and can hurt your career rather than help it. People can hear conviction, or the lack of it, in your voice. Be engaged, be productive, and have fun with the process. Being a change agent is not easy. You will make friends and enemies. Do not confuse friends and enemies with allies. An ally is simply someone who shares a similar value proposition as you do. Much of your time will be spent building strategic alliances that can help your team succeed.

2 EASY EXERCISES TO IMPROVE LISTENING SKILLS

Listening skills are very important. They help us with maintaining good relations with other people. They are also important in business, workplace and classroom.

When you are in meetings or attending an important lecture, here too they play an important role so that you do not miss out on the important points. Many people do not have good listening skills as they do not pay much importance to it. As a result, they find their attention wavering away easily from the current conversation.

SO HOW TO IMPROVE LISTENING SKILLS?

HERE ARE 2 SIMPLE EXERCISES TO IMPROVE LISTENING SKILLS:

1. Whenever you are listening to somebody speak, make it a habit to give oral acknowledgments like 'I see', 'I understand' etc. And then occasionally summarize in your own words what you understood of whatever was said by the other person.

    Summarizing the conversation in your own words every now and then, helps you in two ways. First up, it keeps you actively involved in the conversation thus preventing your attention from wandering away.

    Secondly, it can help in preventing any misunderstandings because if you understood something incorrectly then the speaker can correct you when you are repeating in your words what he/she has said.

2. Ask questions: Ask questions whenever you need clarification for anything or you do not properly understand what was said. Asking questions can help keep the conversation alive, prevent misunderstandings, and also help in developing your listening skills.

    There are a lot of factors which affect how much attention we can pay to the other person. The main thing to remember is that the more actively involved you are in a conversation, the easier it is to pay proper attention to it. You can be actively involved in any conversation by asking relevant questions, discussing your own point of view on the topic, acknowledging and summarizing in your own words etc. The main purpose of all good exercises is to develop in you the active listening.

The above exercises to improve listening skills can be very helpful in keeping your mind alert to what is being said.

DEVELOPING YOUR LISTENING SKILLS

Listening skills are one of the hardest things for language students to develop. This is because good listening ability is something that is usually acquired over long periods of practice and use of the vernacular.

Compared to other areas of language learning, listening skills are complicated by the lack of a structured approach to integrating them into your skillset. Vocabulary, for instance, can be memorized using a variety of mediums, from flash cards to language software. Grammar, on the other hand, is defined by sets of rules that you can follow. For developing speaking and writing skills, there are tons of tried-and-tested exercises that can be employed.

When trying to improve your listening skills, the best thing you can do is to keep getting experience. Watch shows in the language you are studying and try to understand their context. Listen to songs and try to flesh out their meaning .

A lot of the time, it's our own mind that creates problems for our ability to progress in our comprehension abilities. Do you do any of these things that hinder the development of better listening skills?

1. Tuning out. When some students can't understand what they're listening to the first time, they just tend to tune out, their minds either flying out into some other place or their internal dialogues taking over. If you find this behavior becoming a habit, better work to eradicate it. It wastes a lot of your learning time.

2. Letting frustration get the better of you. Many students end up letting frustration at their lack of results get the better of them, often getting angry or just giving up. When you're learning a language, it's

important to understand that not understanding everything is fine -
you will, eventually.

3. Expecting too much. Just like any skill, the development of listening
    skills often occurs at a gradual pace. Don't expect miracles. Instead,
    look towards small improvements that can add up over time.

THEORIES OF PERSONALITY

What is this thing we call personality? Consider the following definitions, what do they have in common?

"Personality is the dynamic organization within the individual of those psychophysical systems that determine his characteristics behavior and though" (Allport, 1961, p. 28).

"The characteristics or blend of characteristics that make a person unique" (Weinberg & Gould, 1999). Both definitions emphasize the uniqueness of the individual and consequently adopt an idiographic view.

The idiographic view assumes that each person has a unique psychological structure and that some traits are possessed by only one person; and that there are times when it is impossible to compare one person with others. It tends to use case studies for information gathering.

The nomothetic view, on the other hand, emphasizes comparability among individuals. This viewpoint sees traits as having the same psychological meaning in everyone. This approach tends to use self-report personality questions, factor analysis, etc. People differ in their positions along a continuum in the same set of traits.

We must also consider the influence and interaction of nature (biology, genetics etc.) and nurture (the environment, upbringing) with respect to personality development.

Trait theories of personality imply personality is biologically based, whereas state theories such as Bandura's (1977) Social Learning Theory emphasize the role of nurture and environmental influence.

Sigmund Freud's psychodynamic theory of personality assumes there is an interaction between nature (innate instincts) and nurture (parental influences).

FREUD'S THEORY

PERSONALITY INVOLVES SEVERAL FACTORS:

– Instinctual drives – food, sex, aggression

– Unconscious processes

– Early childhood influences (re: psychosexual stages) – especially the parents

Personality development depends on the interplay of instinct and environment during the first five years of life. Parental behavior is crucial to normal and abnormal development. Personality and mental health problems in adulthood can usually be traced back to the first five years.

PSYCHOSEXUAL DEVELOPMENT

People – including children – are basically hedonistic – they are driven to seek pleasure by gratifying the Id's desires (Freud, 1920). Sources of pleasure are determined by the location of the libido (life-force).

As a child moves through different developmental stages, the location of the libido, and hence sources of pleasure, change (Freud, 1905).

Environmental and parental experiences during childhood influence an individual's personality during adulthood.

For example, during the first two years of life the infant who is neglected (insufficiently fed) or who is over-protected (over- fed) might become an orally-fixated person (Freud, 1905).

TRIPARTITE THEORY OF PERSONALITY

Freud (1923) saw the personality structured into three parts (i.e. tripartite), the id, ego and superego (also known as the psyche), all developing at different stages in our lives.

These are systems, not parts of the brain, or in any way physical.

The id is the primitive and instinctive component of personality. It consists of all the inherited (i.e. biological) components of personality, including the sex (life) instinct – Eros (which contains the libido), and aggressive (death) instinct - Thanatos.

It operates on the pleasure principle (Freud, 1920) which is the idea that every wishful impulse should be satisfied immediately, regardless of the consequences.

The ego develops in order to mediate between the unrealistic id and the external real world (like a referee). It is the decision making component of personality

The ego operates according to the reality principle, working our realistic ways of satisfying the id's demands, often compromising or postponing satisfaction to avoid negative consequences of society. The ego considers social realities and norms, etiquette and rules in deciding how to behave.

The superego incorporates the values and morals of society which are learned from one's parents and others. It is similar to a conscience, which can punish the ego through causing feelings of guilt.

TRAIT APPROACH TO PERSONALITY

This approach assumes behavior is determined by relatively stable traits which are the fundamental units of one's personality.

Traits predispose one to act in a certain way, regardless of the situation. This means that traits should remain consistent across situations and over time, but may vary between individuals.

It is presumed that individuals differ in their traits due to genetic differences.

These theories are sometimes referred to a psychometric theories, because of their emphasis on measuring personality by using psychometric tests.

EYSENCK'S PERSONALITY THEORY

Eysenck (1952, 1967, 1982) developed a very influential model of personality. Based on the results of factor analyses of responses on personality questionnaires he identified three dimensions of personality: extraversion, neuroticism and psychoticism.

During 1940s Eysenck was working at the Maudsley psychiatric hospital in London. His job was to make an initial assessment of each patient before their mental disorder was diagnosed by a psychiatrist.

Through this position he compiled a battery of questions about behavior, which he later applied to 700 soldiers who were being treated for neurotic disorders at the hospital (Eysenck (1947). He found that the soldiers's answers seemed to link naturally with one another, suggesting that there were a number of different personality traits which were being revealed by the soldier's answers. He called these first order personality traits

He used a technique called factor analysis. This technique reduces behavior to a number of factors which can be grouped together under separate headings, called dimensions.

Eysenck (1947) found that their behavior could be represented by two dimensions: Introversion / Extroversion (E); Neuroticism / Stability (N). Eysenck called these second-order personality traits.

According to Eysenck, the two dimensions of neuroticism (stable vs. unstable) and introversion-extroversion combine to form a variety of personality characteristics.

Extraverts are sociable and crave excitement and change, and thus can become bored easily. They tend to be carefree, optimistic and impulsive.

Introverts are reserved, plan their actions and control their emotions. They tend to be serious, reliable and pessimistic.

Neurotics / unstables tend to be anxious, worrying and moody. They are overly emotional and find it difficult to calm down once upset.

Stables are emotionally calm, unreactive and unworried.

Eysenck (1966) later added a third trait / dimension - Psychoticism – e.g. lacking in empathy, cruel, a loner, aggressive and troublesome.

Eysenck related the personality of an individual to the functioning of the autonomic nervous system (ANS). Personality is dependent on the balance between excitation and inhibition process of the nervous system. Neurotic individuals have an ANS that responds quickly to stress.

CATTELL'S 16PF TRAIT THEORY

Cattell (1965) disagreed with Eysenck's view that personality can be understood by looking at only two or three dimensions of behavior.

Instead, he argued that that is was necessary to look at a much larger number of traits in order to get a complete picture of someone's personality.

Whereas Eysenck based his theory based on the responses of hospitalized servicemen, Cattell collected data from a range of people through three different sources of data.

* L-data - this is life record data such as school grades, absence from work etc.

* Q-data - this was a questionnaire designed to rate an individual's personality.

* T-data - this is data from objective tests designed to 'tap' into a personality construct.

Cattell analyzed the T-data and Q-data using a mathematical technique called factor analysis to look at which types of behavior tended to be grouped together in the same people. He identified 16 personality traits / factors common to all people.

Cattell made a distinction between source and surface traits. Surface traits are very obvious and can be easily identified by other people, whereas source traits are less visible to other people and appear to underlie several different aspects of behavior.

Cattell regarded source traits are more important in describing personality than surface traits.

Cattell produced a personality test similar to the EPI that measured each of the sixteen traits. The 16PF (16 Personality Factors Test) has 160 questions in total, 10 questions relating to each personality factor.

ALLPORT'S TRAIT THEORY

Allport's theory of personality emphasizes the uniqueness of the individual and the internal cognitive and motivational processes that influence behavior. For example, intelligence, temperament, habits, skills, attitudes, and traits.

Allport (1937) believes that personality is biologically determined at birth, and shaped by a person's environmental experience.

CRITICAL EVALUATION OF TRAIT THEORIES

Twin studies can be used to see if personality is genetic. However, the findings are conflicting and non-conclusive.

Shields (1976) found that monozygotic (identical) twins were significantly more alike on the Introvert – Extrovert (E) and Psychoticism (P) dimensions than dizygotic (non-identical) twins.

Loehlin, Willerman and Horn (1988) found that only 50% of the variations of scores on personality dimensions are due to inherited traits. This suggests that social factors are also important.

AUTHORITARIAN PERSONALITY

Adorno et al. (1950) proposed that prejudice is the results of an individual's personality type. They piloted and developed a questionnaire, which they called the F-scale (F for fascism).

Adorno argued that deep-seated personality traits predisposed some individuals to be highly sensitive to totalitarian and antidemocratic ideas and therefore were prone to be highly prejudicial.

The evidence they gave to support this conclusion included:

- Case studies, e.g. Nazis

- Psychometric testing (use of the F-scale)

- Clinical interviews revealed situational aspects of their childhood, such as the fact that they had been brought up by very strict parents or guardians, which were found of participants who scored highly on the F-scale not always found in the backgrounds of low scorers.

Those with an authoritarian personality tended to be:

- Hostile to those who are of inferior status, but obedient of people with high status

- Fairly rigid in their opinions and beliefs

- Conventional, upholding traditional values

Adorno concluded that people with authoritarian personalities were more likely to categorize people into "us" and "them" groups, seeing their own group as superior.

Therefore, the study indicated that individuals with a very strict upbringing by critical and harsh parents were most likely to develop an authoritarian personality.

Adorno believed that this was because the individual in question was not able to express hostility towards their parents (for being strict and critical). Consequently, the person would then displace this aggression / hostility onto safer targets, namely those who are weaker, such as ethnic minorities.

Adorno et al. felt that authoritarian traits, as identified by the F-Scale, predispose some individuals towards 'fascistic' characteristics such as:

- Ethnocentrism, i.e. the tendency to favor one's own ethnic group:

- Obsession with rank and status

- Respect for and submissiveness to authority figures

- Preoccupation with power and toughness.

In other words, according to Adorno, the Eichmanns of this world are there because they have authoritarian personalities and therefore are predisposed cruelty, as a result of their upbringing.

There is evidence that the authoritarian personality exists. This might help to explain why some people are more resistant to changing their prejudiced views.

CRITICAL EVALUATION

There are many weaknesses in Adorno's explanation of prejudice:

- Harsh parenting style does not always produce prejudice children / individuals

- Some prejudice people do not conform to the authoritarian personality type.

- Doesn't explain why people are prejudiced against certain groups and not others.

Furthermore, the authoritarian explanation of prejudice does not explain how whole social groups (e.g. the Nazis) can be prejudiced. This would mean that all members of a group (e.g. Nazis) would have an authoritarian personality, which is quite unlikely.

Cultural or social norms would seem to offer a better explanation of prejudice and conflict than personality variables. Adorno has also been criticized for his limited sample.

Also, Hyman and Sheatsley (1954) found that lower educational level was probably a better explanation of high F-scale scores than an authoritarian.

WHAT IS BODY LANGUAGE? THE MISSING INGREDIENT

People are constantly throwing off a storm of signals. These signals may be silent (non-verbal) messages communicated through the sender's body movements, facial expressions, voice tone and loudness. Microexpressions, hand gestures, and posture register almost immediately, a silent orchestra that can have long-lasting repercussions.

"What do you read my lord?" "Words," said Hamlet. Methinks he should hath answered "body language." Where many of us are obsessed with words, always thinking of what we'll say next, we pay comparatively little attention to our body language. Strange given that 55% of communication is conveyed through body language and only 7% involves words.

Take a moment to consider that fact. 7% of communication is words. 55% is body language. It is a staggering fact, a fact that makes one thing clear: if you are to make the most of your communication skills--social, professional or wherever else--you need to make use of body language.

How, then, can you begin, today, right now, to take advantage of that whopping great 55% of communication that comes from body language? There are a great many ways. Let's take a look at some of the most popular and most important.

Conflict Resolution: Perhaps you are one of the unfortunate people who seem to get in arguments often without much of a clue why. Some people seem to create conflict seemingly out of thin air. A certain guy who shall remain unnamed but who serves as a perfect example is continually getting in arguments. He speaks politely. He never says a word wrong, yet he keeps getting in arguments. Why? Because he has nervous body language. He folds his arms over his chest. He rarely if ever smiles. He'll tap on a table or other object while he speaks. His words remain polite, but his body language is anything but. His body language passes from irritated to aggressive to impatient perpetually.

If you are one of the unlucky ones who, like our example man, gets into arguments seemingly from nowhere, be sure to check yourself for the following negative gestures

* Do not cross your arms over your chest

* Do not tap on objects

* Do not fidget with your hair or face

* Smile and nod occasionally to let your company know you are happy and agreeable

There are more gestures we could cover here, but the purpose is not to give an absolute blueprint to positive body language, rather it is to make one point clear: if you get into arguments you can't find reason for in your words, look to your body language. This is likely the cause of the conflict. A few simple corrective measures here and there will see those arguments turned to happy conversation.

BODY LANGUAGE IN DATING:

Romance is likely the number one reason people learn about body language. It's a wise step. That 55% of communication counts in romance just as in general everyday conversation. Using positive and strong nonverbals can do an amazing job of presenting yourself as an attractive and, importantly, approachable person.

Here are some suggestions of how to use nonverbal communication to attract people.

Do not smile to often, but when you met someone new show them a genuine smile to show that you really are happy to have met them. Make a habit of this. That way, when you meet someone you like you'll be certain to give a good first impression, saying, "Oh, wow, I like you. I'm very happy we met." Said in words, this sentence means little, but when you say it through your body it is a powerful communicator, one which will get a relationship off to a great start.

Stand with your legs hip with apart: Some alleged specialists will advice men to stand with their legs far apart to show dominance that attracts women. The problem, with this is that guys overdo it. They turn a simple pose into a comically exaggerated spectacle of their crown jewels. Just stand with your legs comfortably apart, this will show confidence and strength.

Long Gazes: Nervous guys and girls will see a person they are attracted to look away shyly. Big mistake. This gives the impression that a) you're weak and b) you don't like the person you looked at (because, logic would dictate, if you enjoyed looking at them you would continue to do so).

Again, basic steps; you'll find that little corrective moves like this make all the difference.

Let's look at one more area where nonverbal communication is important.

FRIENDLINESS:

Here are some suggestions to help you show friendliness through nonverbal communication while still looking dominant and strong.

Smile just enough to let people know you're happy but do not overdo it

If you have a habit of fiddling with objects or fidgeting with yourself stop it, it makes your company think you're fed up or bored with them.

When you stand, do not cover up your throat, chest, stomach or privates with any barriers (a barrier might include your arms, a purse, an item you are carrying or anything else which gets in the way).

Point your feet and belly button towards the other person. This shows a great deal of interest in them. It will come across as a compliment and be greatly received.

These are but a selection of the many ways in which nonverbal communication can have influence in your life. This section of the eBook has illustrated how you can begin to use simple gestures today to boost your communication skills and to create more positive relationships. Use them and see how much of an improvement you notice in your communications. I am confident you will be pleasantly surprised.

HELPING TO UNDERSTAND BODY LANGUAGE RE: LYING, DATING AND JOB INTERVIEWS

Your body language says a lot about you and has a major impact on how others see you. As such you can learn a lot from the body language of others.

Body language accounts for up to 55% of how we communicate. Body language along with verbal cues can indicate a number of different things depending on the context. People with powerful body language with open movements that take up more space tend to feel more confident. They are more likely to have less stress, be more dominant, take more risks and be more optimistic. Dominant body language creates a powerful appearance. Studies show that even faking high and low poses effected the confidence level of the participants both positively and negatively.

The idea of fake it til you make it may seem false, but in faking it the process will help you become it starting with small changes to your body language. Something everyone can learn.

Here are three common situations in which body language is especially important - a job interview, dating and detecting lies, and ways to read between the lines to help understand what is really going on.

Like it or not we all lie a lot. When conversing with a stranger we are likely to lie once or more in the first 10 minutes. They may be little lies but we still do it. Most of us will participate in deception from time to time to avoid conflict, but we are probably better off telling the truth. Words can be deceptive but the human body has a hard time hiding lies. Using your own body language and being able to read body language of others can be extremely useful when communicating with others.

THE BASICS OF BODY LANGUAGE:

Your primary goal when reading body language is to determine their comfort level in their current situation. There is a process of combining verbal cues and body language to determine this.

POSITIVE BODY LANGUAGE:

* Moving or leaning closer to you

* Relaxed, uncrossed limbs

* Long periods of eye contact

* Looking down and away out of shyness

* Genuine Smiles

NEGATIVE BODY LANGUAGE:

* Moving or leaning away from you

* Crossed arms or legs

* Looking away to the side

* Feet pointed away from you, or towards an exit

* Rubbing/scratching their nose, eyes, or the back of their neck

A single cue can be misleading so it's essential to pay attention to multiple behavioral cues.

LYING:

Being able to judge whether someone is lying through reading their Body Language is a big advantage. Your intuition is never 100% accurate, but with practice you can become more aware of when you're being lied to. This technique will help with the big lies but it's very difficult to detect white lies, lies of omission or exaggeration.

Research has shown that liars often exhibit much of the uncomfortable behavior plus some specific additional traits.

FAKE SMILES

Research has shown it is almost impossible to fake a genuine smile when lying. This is why many people appear awkward in family photos. The smiles look awkward if they are faking it. Your genuine smile is in the eyes as your smile pushes up your cheeks and creates wrinkles around your eyes. It is difficult to fake this as you need to feel some genuine happy emotion to do it and that is almost impossible if you are lying. So a fake smile is helpful in determining if a lie is in progress.

TOO MUCH EYE CONTACT AND A STIFF UPPER BODY

Often a liar will overcompensate with too much eye contact, and appear stiff while they try not to fidget, this can make you feel uncomfortable and unsettled. In genuine conversations people move and do not hold eye contact for long periods. Liars because they are uncomfortable will often rub their neck or eyes and look away to the side and opt to do little. If you notice tense shoulders and a high amount of eye contact you likely talking to a liar..

VERBAL CUES

Pay attention to the conversation, liars will offer more details and suggest punishments for the real offenders if they are being accused of something. They will answer your questions with a question giving them time to make up an answer. This type of conversation paired with negative body language points to dishonesty.

It's important to realize that some people may always behave awkwardly. Look for multiple cues and trust your instincts and ask for verification if you just aren't sure.

DATING:

On the first date understanding your date's body language is incredibly helpful in knowing when not to talk about something that makes them uncomfortable.

Basically you are just looking for general indications of comfort and discomfort. This means paying attention to how guarded their body language is. On a first date most people will be fairly guarded crossing their arms, keeping a distance and keeping their palms face upwards. Your goal is to encourage them to be more open by being more open and welcoming yourself with uncrossed arms and a warm genuine smile. We all tend to mimic the behavior of others so if you're warm and comfortable it will help them become more comfortable.

Comfort levels can fluctuate on a first date as they are nerve-wracking, and you are likely to make a few mistakes. Don't worry just keep going. Watch for positive body language and focus on what brings that out. If you witness negative body language change the subject. Of course there will be evenings when you just don't jibe with the other person and there will be many awkward periods. If this happens know that person wasn't for you and move on.

JOB INTERVIEWS:

Job interviews are similar to first dates except that on a date you are on an equal basis whereas in a job interview the interviewer has the power. This creates a situation were you are more uncomfortable than the interviewer. You could easily display negative body language which you need to override in order not to appear closed off.

FIRST IMPRESSIONS

First impressions do count so a smile, a handshake and a warm greeting along with the previously mentioned positive body language will bode you well for a comfortable interview.

Go into the interview prepared, this will increase your comfort level and add to your confidence level. To prepare research the company and any individuals that may be interviewing you.

Natural comfort is your most valuable tool, however there some tricks to help you enhance your comfort. Eye contact is important especially when asking questions and when the interviewer has something to tell you. Avoid blocking your eyes, lean slightly forward, and appear to be a good listener by placing your hand over your mouth indicating you are not going to talk and are paying attention.

Any reasonable Interviewer will understand that you are a little nervous and tense. In fact if you're overconfident it can indicate that you are not taking the interview seriously.

Understanding body language along with verbal cues can be useful in communicating and understanding others. It can be fun, but you're not a psychic, you can't read minds or interpret what someone is thinking or feeling. Use these techniques to find clues to help you understand other people and communicate better.

THE BENEFITS AND CONSEQUENCES OF EFFICIENT BODY LANGUAGE

WHAT MORE CAN YOU ACCOMPLISH WITH EFFICIENT BODY LANGUAGE?

Have you ever wondered what kind of information is available from your body, how important it is and who can read it? Did you know there is now a growing interest in profiting from learning to interpret this overlooked area of human behavior? What are the benefits and the consequences of this trend?

Efficient body language compliments efficient organizations

One of the major focal points of the Information Age has been on streamlining operations and making organizations efficient. With the ubiquitous use of spreadsheets and management software hardly any business process has not been scrutinized and re-engineered. Although much time, energy and frustration have been saved incorporating machines and computers into our lives and work, this intense focus on technological solutions may have made us blind to the information our bodies incorporate and express. Our body language can and often does contradict and even sabotage what our well-rehearsed mouths are communicating. Yet how aware are you of it when it occurs?

THE POWER AND PROMISE OF GRAVITY

For instance, observe how efficient is the average person's relationship with gravity. Most of us take this incredible attracting force for granted. Indeed, who has time to care about gravity when there are bills to pay, products to sell and people to meet? Yet, think about how powerful the pull of gravity is when it comes to holding our world together. It even holds our moon in place. You are then welcome to marvel at the incredible amount of energy many of us use to resist this unavoidable force. For just a moment think about how much better we could feel and how much more energy we would have, how much better we could express ourselves just by being conscious of and working a little more in line with the Force of Gravity?

Most of us pay little or no conscious attention to the level of efficiency we use aligning our posture with gravity's pull. Since curiosity is an unavoidable part of human nature, it was only a matter of time before focus returned to profiting from more efficient use of the body's language. What if that time is now here?

READING BODY LANGUAGE BASICS

Take a walk in a crowded place and observe your fellow humans and how they use their posture to:

- Walk or stand while leaning forward, backward or to one side and work against gravity.

- Hang their heads forward or backward conspicuously out of line with their center of gravity,

- Rock or waddle from side to side while walking forward.

- Aim their feet in another direction than the one they are walking towards.

- Wave their arms around much more than just to maintain their balance

- Shuffle so much when they walk that their shoes begin wearing unevenly?

Each one of these nonessential movements requires energy and effort to purposefully counteract the force that gravity imposes upon them. Also notice that small children use gravity most efficiently, yet as we age and become smarter we tend to ignore gravity's pull more and more. Using one's own energy to resist gravity is totally unnecessary and insane if we are really trying to use our energy efficiently. If we are that blind to what our bodies are doing when it comes to our posture what kind of effect, conscious or unconscious, can this behavior have on those with whom we are communicating?

THE LIGHT'S ON AND NOBODY'S HOME

Pay attention to how most of us seem oblivious to what our bodies are doing while we go about our day. Many of these movements are the product of being unconscious of our body language or being conditioned by society to ignore it. Regardless of the benefit or consequence, do something often enough and you will create a behavior pattern. Once a pattern is in place it doesn't take long to become part of your identity. For most of us this pattern becomes incorporated into who they think they are. Even with an injury, if the initial pain you wanted to avoid disappears, the pattern and muscle tension is often forgotten and remains. Many go further by wasting even more energy and time by complaining about how tired they feel.

Does this sound like efficient use of our resources?

EFFICIENT BODY LANGUAGE IS OFTEN UNWELCOME INFORMATION

You are now invited to try informing someone of your observations. If you actually dare to take on this challenge, marvel at the responses you get. Most will politely excuse it away, often blaming an old injury. Others will become insulted that you would bring this up as this is "just the way they are." Note closely how many warmly thank you for your advice and begin immediately adjusting these inefficiencies. If knowledge is power, do you also sense an opportunity to learn something most others ignore.

REFLECTING OVER CONSCIOUS AND EFFICIENT BODY LANGUAGE

Most importantly, you are invited to reflect over what people's' body language, behavior patterns and their responses to your comments tell you about the individuals involved.

- Do these patterns make them appear more or less attractive?

- Would you be more or less inclined to hire them?

- Are you more or less interested in their advice?

- Does their age and intelligence seem to affect how they respond to you?

- Would you wish someone in your family to show these patterns or date someone who does?

As a bonus, ask yourself what does their response tell you about their ability to be curious, adaptive and responsive?

What about your own Body Language Signals?

So far we have talked about all of those other people surrounding you. Here is your invitation to stand in front of a mirror, take a reflective inventory on all the questions above and see how they relate to you and your body language. What does your body language say? How quick are you to acknowledge and adjust it? By the way, how many of those around you may also know how to read it?

THE PROFIT IN UNDERSTANDING CONSCIOUS BODY LANGUAGE

There is a gold mine here waiting for those who understand how to read, feel and interpret what the body language of another is demonstrating. There is also a jackpot waiting for those who are aware of what their own body language is saying. There is a third jackpot waiting for those who understand that by adjusting theirs they will not only feel healthier and happier, they will become more attractive and influential. Could your body language have something to do with your success?

HOW TO READ PEOPLE LIKE AN FBI PROFILER

What do you make of a neighbor who's married, has kids, dresses in a suit daily, rarely misses a day of work, has a well- groomed lawn and a tidy home, is friendly and polite, always asks about your day and your children, and even shovels your snow when you're out of town? Most people would think this is the best neighbor on the block.

So you may be surprised to learn that this very neighbor "was a sexual sadist who was using a small trailer in this backyard as a torture chamber," write Mary Ellen O'Toole and Alisa Bowman in their book Dangerous Instincts: How Gut Instincts Betray Us. O'Toole, a retired FBI profiler, worked the case and interviewed the 60-year-old park ranger David Parker Ray, who appeared charming and even seemed to admire women. As it turned out, he'd been torturing women in his backyard for years, and none of his neighbors ever suspected him to be anything but a "regular guy."

When we try to determine whether someone is a good person or a potential threat, we tend to focus on superficial qualities that actually don't tell us much about the individual. We assume that people who go to work every day, have a family and a well-kept home are normal—and we give them a lot of credibility, O'Toole said.

We also assume that our bodies will warn us when we're around someone dangerous. We'll experience the sensations of fear and know to stay away. But as O'Toole said, dangerous people have a way of making us feel very comfortable. For instance, they're friendly and courteous and make good eye contact. When O'Toole first saw David Parker Ray, he took her hand and told her how nice it was to meet her. He also was polite and well-mannered. Even O'Toole, who's worked on the most notorious criminal cases, had to keep reminding herself of his heinous crimes.

What also complicates our ability to read people accurately is that many of us aren't good listeners. The best way to tell if someone is dangerous is by observing their behavior, O'Toole said. That's what FBI profilers do. "In order to be a good reader of behavior, you have to watch and listen," O'Toole said. But if you're too busy talking the whole time, you may miss key pieces of information.

We also tend to admire and even get intimidated by people in certain professions and positions, which additionally hampers our judgment. O'Toole calls this "icon-intimidation." We automatically give people a pass if they're a religious figure, police officer or military person. We assign admirable qualities to them without much thought. We assume they're intelligent, courageous, compassionate and thereby harmless.

O'Toole gave the example of a recent case in Washington D.C. The area offers a free carpooling service called Slugging, where people give strangers a ride into the city. Last year two commuters got into a pricey car with a retired high-ranking military officer. After they got in, he started driving 90 mph. The people were terrified and insisted on being let out of the car.

Once out, one of the people tried to take a picture of his license plate. He tried to run them over.

When reading others, people also "are clouded by their own emotional state," O'Toole said. Being depressed or just losing a loved one puts you in a vulnerable state when someone offers to do something nice for you, she said.

In our society, we also hold onto many myths that put us in danger. O'Toole calls one of the most common myths "the myth of the straggly-haired stranger." That is, we think that dangerous people look creepy, unkempt, are unemployed and uneducated and basically stick out like sore thumbs. So we overlook people who may be incredibly dangerous because they look like the rest of us.

Another myth is that good people just snap and act violently, O'Toole said. However, individuals who "snap" already have traits that predispose them to violence, such as a short fuse or physical aggression. It's more likely, she added, that people minimize the presence of these red flags and that's why it seems so unexpected.

In fact, it's common for people to minimize danger in general. We may choose to ignore certain patterns of behavior, rationalize them, explain them away or talk ourselves out of taking action, O'Toole said. Take the example of a couple where one partner becomes increasingly obsessive and jealous (and even physically abusive), which O'Toole commonly sees as a consultant to schools and universities. The young woman wants to end the relationship, but she's afraid of him. He has many good friends, plays competitive sports and comes from a well-to-do family. She doesn't want to get him in trouble and worries that their friends will hate her. So the parents decide to deal with the situation on their own. They underestimate the danger. But these are criminal behaviors and they don't just begin in young adulthood, O'Toole said. It's likely he's done similar things with other girls and has other concerning traits. Just getting your daughter out of this situation is not enough, and it "could cause your daughter to lose her life."

RED FLAGS WHEN READING PEOPLE

Again, reading people accurately means going beyond superficial traits and observing their behaviors. According to O'Toole, these are several red flags of concerning or dangerous actions.

THEY ANGER EASILY OR TALK ABOUT VIOLENCE.

A person who has a short fuse in one situation will usually have it in another. For instance, if a person has road rage, it's a good indicator that they also have anger problems outside the car, O'Toole said. Another red flag is if they think that "violence is the answer to everything no matter what they're talking about."

THEY ARE PHYSICALLY AGGRESSIVE OR ABUSIVE TO OTHERS.

Has the person ever been physically aggressive with you or others? How do they treat staff or servers at a restaurant? If they mistreat others or act like a bully, this likely spills over into other areas of their life, O'Toole said.

THEY TEND TO BLAME OTHERS.

Let's say you're on your first or second date with a person, and they mention their past relationships. They not only have nothing good to say about their previous partners, but they blame them for everything, she said.

THEY LACK EMPATHY OR COMPASSION.

O'Toole views a lack of empathy and compassion as important indicators of someone's character and their dangerousness. You can identify whether someone is empathetic or compassionate in a simple conversation, and in as little as 10 minutes, O'Toole said. These individuals highjack conversations by interrupting and refocusing the talk back to them.

Again, take the example of a blind date. The person not only blames their past partners for everything, but they may speak harshly about them or even make fun of their physical appearance, O'Toole said.

Psychopaths, who make up about one percent of the general population and 10 percent of prisoners, also lack empathy (among meeting other criteria). They may pretend as though they care, empathize and have feelings for their victims. But, as O'Toole and Bowman write in Dangerous Instincts, "Asking a psychopath what remorse or guilt feels like is like asking a man what it feels like to be pregnant. It is an experience they have never had." If you keep asking a psychopath about their feelings (such as "How do you feel about those victims?"), they'll become irritated, and their façade will start to crack, O'Toole said. For psychopaths, "emotions are a pain in their rear end." They see them as problems, not something worth having.

Reading people accurately isn't a gift; it's a skill that anyone can master if they start paying attention to the right things.